EXPLORE THE U.S.A.

PUERTO RICO

Helen Lepp Friesen

Go to **www.av2books.com**,
and enter this book's
unique code.

BOOK CODE

M 5 6 0 0 8 2

AV² by Weigl brings you media
enhanced books that support
active learning.

AV² provides enriched content that supplements and complements this book. Weigl's AV² books
strive to create inspired learning and engage young minds in a total learning experience.

Your AV² Media Enhanced books come alive with...

 Audio
Listen to sections of
the book read aloud.

 Video
Watch informative
video clips.

 Embedded Weblinks
Gain additional information
for research.

 Try This!
Complete activities and
hands-on experiments.

 Key Words
Study vocabulary, and
complete a matching
word activity.

 Quizzes
Test your knowledge.

 Slide Show
View images and
captions, and prepare
a presentation.

...and much, much more!

Published by AV² by Weigl
350 5th Avenue, 59th Floor
New York, NY 10118
Website: www.av2books.com   www.weigl.com

Library of Congress Cataloging-in-Publication Data
Friesen, Helen Lepp, 1961-
Puerto Rico / Helen Lepp Friesen.
    p. cm. -- (Explore the U.S.A.)
Includes bibliographical references and index.
Audience: Grades K-3.
ISBN 978-1-61913-397-6 (hbk. : alk. paper)
1. Puerto Rico--Juvenile literature. I. Title.
F1958.3.F75 2013
972.95--dc23
                      2012015938

Printed in the United States of America in North Mankato, Minnesota
1 2 3 4 5 6 7 8 9 16 15 14 13 12

052012
WEP040512

Project Coordinator: Karen Durrie
Art Director: Terry Paulhus

Weigl acknowledges Getty Images as the primary
image supplier for this title.

PUERTO RICO

Contents

3

This is Puerto Rico.
It is called the Isle of Enchantment.
Puerto Rico is a tropical island.

This is the shape of Puerto Rico. Puerto Rico is made up of one large island and many small ones.

Where is Puerto Rico?

Canada

United States

Pacific Ocean

Mexico

Gulf of Mexico

Atlantic Ocean

Caribbean Sea

Puerto Rico is in the Caribbean Sea.

People called the Tainos lived in Puerto Rico more than 800 years ago. The Tainos were good farmers and sailors.

The Tainos lived in big round houses where 10 to 15 families could stay.

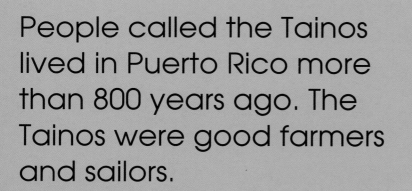

The hibiscus is the Puerto Rico flower. It has leaves shaped like hearts.

The Puerto Rico seal has a lamb, a castle, and a lion.

The castle and lion stand for Spain.

This is the flag of Puerto Rico. It has five stripes. Three stripes are red, and two are white.

The flag also has a white star on a blue triangle.

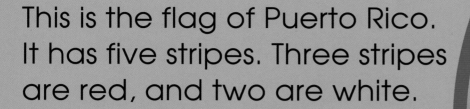

The state animal of Puerto Rico is the coqui frog. Its name comes from the sound it makes.

Coqui frogs are about 1 inch long.

This is the biggest city in Puerto Rico. It is called San Juan. It is the capital city of Puerto Rico.

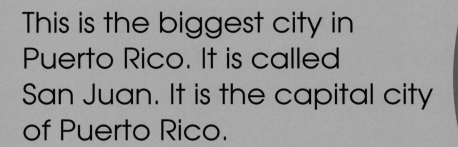

San Juan is the oldest city in the United States.

Bananas grow in Puerto Rico.
A banana bunch is called a hand.
One person in the United States
eats about 27 pounds of bananas
each year.

Puerto Rico has about
4,000 banana farms.

Puerto Rico is known for its warm weather and beautiful sandy beaches.

People come to swim, surf, and visit Old San Juan.

PUERTO RICO FACTS

These pages provide detailed information that expands on the interesting facts found in the book. These pages are intended to be used by adults as a learning support to help young readers round out their knowledge of each state in the *Explore the U.S.A.* series.

Pages 4–5

Puerto Rico is not attached to mainland North America. In 1898, the United States took control of Puerto Rico, but it is not a state like the other states. Puerto Rico is a commonwealth. This means that it is similar to a state, but its people may not vote for the U.S. president. Puerto Rico's main language is Spanish. The name *Puerto Rico* means "rich port" in Spanish.

Pages 6–7

Puerto Rico is a group of islands in the northeast Caribbean Sea. The main island is called Puerto Rico. The other islands are Vieques, Culebra, Mona, and several smaller islands. Puerto Rico is located 1,000 miles (1,600 kilometers) southeast of Florida. The Dominican Republic is to the west, and the U.S. Virgin Islands are to the east.

Pages 8–9

Native people lived in Puerto Rico long before European settlers arrived. In 1492, Christopher Columbus was one of the first Europeans to land in Puerto Rico. Over the next 300 years, the Spanish used Puerto Rico as a port on their way to Mexico, Cuba, and South America. After their loss in the Spanish–American War of 1898, the Spanish granted ownership of Puerto Rico to the United States.

Pages 10–11

Hibiscus bloom year-round in Puerto Rico because of the warm weather. The letters 'F' and 'I' on the Puerto Rico seal stand for Fernando and Isabel. They were the Spanish king and queen when the island was named. The Latin words on the seal mean "Juan is its name." Puerto Rico was first called San Juan. Now, San Juan is the name of the capital city. The seal's castles, crosses, and lions represent Puerto Rico's Spanish roots.

Pages 12–13

The Puerto Rico flag is always flown with the U.S. flag in Puerto Rico. The white star represents the commonwealth. The triangle stands for the three government branches. Three red stripes represent the blood that supports the government. Two white stripes stand for freedom and rights.

Pages 14–15

The small coqui frog has a little tail when it is born. The tail falls off soon after birth. Coqui frogs may be yellow, green, or brown. They have pads on their toes that help them stick to leaves. The coqui males sing when the Sun goes down.

Pages 16–17

San Juan is the capital of Puerto Rico. The Spanish founded the city in 1521. They built a thick wall around the city to protect it from their enemies. Most of the population is of Hispanic descent. More than 420,000 people live in San Juan. San Juan means Saint John.

Pages 18–19

More than 770,000 bananas and plantains are grown in Puerto Rico each year. Plantains are related to the banana. However, plantains are more starchy and less sweet than bananas. Both fruits grow year-round in Puerto Rico. Other important food crops include coffee, sugar cane, and pineapple.

Pages 20–21

Puerto Rico has warm weather year-round, more than 300 miles (483 km) of beaches, and a rich culture. Most visitors come from the United States because American citizens do not need a passport to visit. More than 400 restored historic buildings from the 16th and 17th centuries are in Old San Juan. Puerto Rico's El Yunque National Forest is the only tropical rainforest in the United States.

KEY WORDS

Research has shown that as much as 65 percent of all written material published in English is made up of 300 words. These 300 words cannot be taught using pictures or learned by sounding them out. They must be recognized by sight. This book contains 53 common sight words to help young readers improve their reading fluency and comprehension. This book also teaches young readers several important content words, such as proper nouns. These words are paired with pictures to aid in learning and improve understanding.

Page	Sight Words First Appearance
4	a, is, it, this, the
7	and, in, large, made, many, of, one, small, up, where
8	big, could, good, houses, lived, more, people, than, to, were, where, years
11	for, has, leaves, like
12	also, are, on, three, two, white
15	about, animal, comes, from, its, long, makes, name, sound
16	city
19	each, eats, farms, grow, hand
20	old

Page	Content Words First Appearance
4	island, Isle of Enchantment, Puerto Rico
7	Caribbean Sea, shape
8	farmers, sailors, Tainos
11	castle, flower, hearts, hibiscus, lamb, lion, seal, Spain
12	flag, star, stripes, triangle
15	coqui frog, inch
16	San Juan
19	bananas, bunch, pounds, United States
20	beaches, weather

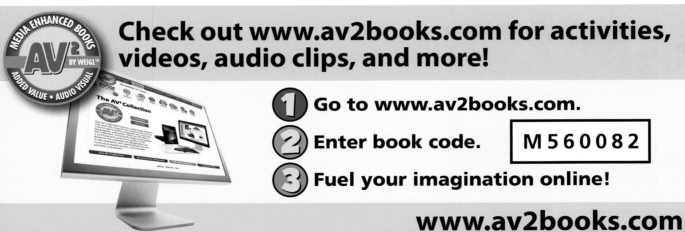